Protocols for Professional Learning Conversations

Cultivating the Art and Discipline

A Joint Publication

Solution Tree   Connections Publishing

Protocols for Professional Learning Conversations

Cultivating the Art and Discipline

Catherine Glaude, Ph.D.

Published in the US by Solution Tree Press

555 North Morton Street

Bloomington, IN 47404

800.733.6786 (toll free) / 812.336.7700

FAX: 812.336.7790

email: info@solution-tree.com

solution-tree.com

Printed in the United States of America

15 14 13 12 11   1 2 3 4 5

FSC

Mixed Sources

Product group from well-managed
forests and other controlled sources

Cert no. SW-COC-002283
www.fsc.org
© 1996 Forest Stewardship Council

Library of Congress Cataloging-in-Publication Data

Glaude, Catherine.

 Protocols for professional learning conversations : cultivating the art and discipline / Catherine Glaude. -- 1st us ed.

    p. cm.

 Includes bibliographical references.

 ISBN 978-1-935543-82-4 (perfect bound) -- ISBN 978-1-935543-83-1 (library edition)

 1. Education. 2. School personnel management--United States. 3. Academic achievement. I. Title.

 LB1025.3.G55 2011

 370--dc22

                    2011008105

Solution Tree

Jeffrey C. Jones, CEO & President

Solution Tree Press

President: Douglas M. Rife

Publisher: Robert D. Clouse

Vice President of Production: Gretchen Knapp

Managing Production Editor: Caroline Wise

Senior Production Editor: Risë Koben

Connections Publishing

Stewart Duncan, CEO & President

Project Manager: Judith Hall-Patch

Editor: Annie Jack

Design: Anthony Alexander, Beachwalker Studio, Cori Jones

Dedication

To my colleagues in Yarmouth, Maine, who inspire me with their
dedication for improving student learning and offer me a rich garden
to grow my skills as facilitator

Table of Contents

Foreword

In 1996, I was first introduced to a protocol when reading an issue of *Horace* from the Coalition of Essential Schools. The protocol was a simple one in which a presenting teacher offered student work for feedback from colleagues. I tried this protocol with some courageous presenters and several groups of educators and was intrigued by what I discovered. The protocol promoted calmer, more thoughtful dialogues than ones I had previously experienced. I saw the "structured time to listen" allowing for a safe exchange of ideas and encouraging deep listening. The "warm and cool" feedback, as the protocol named it, helped teachers identify areas of strengths and where questions or challenges were seen.

Since 1996, I have continued to collect and use protocols from a variety of sources. I soon discovered that some individuals were more skillful in receiving feedback and learning with others. I began to see some patterns in development. I noticed that learning focused on a common reading from a text was not as threatening as learning focused on student work; that some individuals embraced the use of protocols while others resisted them; that some individuals needed more support when using a protocol than others; that some schools embraced protocols more rapidly than other schools; and that some individuals were more comfortable in modifying protocols. These observations lead me to believe that using protocols is developmental and that the culture of the school plays an important role in this development.

As my collection of protocols continued to grow, I found more and more opportunities for using them in my work and began creating or adapting protocols to fit specific purposes. I found if I started with the end in mind and thought about the time limits and specific behaviors I needed to promote, I could easily create a protocol. Debriefing at the end of the protocol was essential since it often sparked ideas for improvements.

I encourage you to start or continue your journey in using protocols. I hope the ones I offer you may be used or adapted to fit your purposes or they may inspire you to create your own.

SECTION 1

What Is a Professional Learning Conversation?

Collegial workplaces depend on teachers' openness and readiness to improve. They must have reference groups of peers for identifying problems and taking action; ample time for observations and discussions; and administrators who both encourage teachers and accommodate their needs as they explore new collegial relationships.

—Susan Moore Johnson

What Is a Professional Learning Conversation?

The goal of a learning conversation is to improve student learning. Collectively, educators possess a wealth of knowledge, skills, and experiences that are invaluable resources to each other. When the focus is on improving student learning, educators need each other to consider and inspect their practices against the current research. There is much to be learned from these collaborative conversations. Structured, ongoing learning dialogue can be the most powerful professional development an educator will experience.

Why Use a Protocol?

A protocol is a process for guiding a professional learning conversation. The purpose of a protocol is to build the skills and promote the culture necessary for ongoing collaborative learning.

A protocol:

1. Keeps a group conversation focused in order to generate a wealth of helpful conversation and feedback in a limited amount of time

2. Encourages all members of the group to offer their most thoughtful and useful feedback and/or insights on a specific topic

3. Helps less verbal participants offer their voices into the conversation

4. Promotes thoughtfulness by allowing personal reflecting time within a group conversation

5. Encourages lively dialogue featuring multiple perspectives

6. Requires any individuals presenting their personal work to remain silent so that the feedback and insights offered from their colleagues are not lost

7. Reminds individuals to return to the evidence offered in the text or the video, rather than offering opinions, when conversations are focused on current research

8. Provides a safe and supportive structure for all to inspect their practices and results of the learning

Where Do You Start With Protocols?

Building a professional learning community takes time. The more directed a learning conversation is to an individual's practice, the more threatening it may become. However, the threat is replaced with enthusiasm about improving student learning when focused conversations become the norm and individuals become skillful in learning together. Protocols enable the dialogue.

Using protocols to promote dialogue around a common reading assignment is less threatening than conversations focused on personal practice and student work. The protocols in the beginning of this resource book are a good starting point for building skills and creating a climate for learning together. Protocols at the end of this resource book are provided for use when skills and a culture exist to support collaborative work focused on improving individual practice.

Why Use Ground Rules?

In addition to the protocol, key tools you need to navigate a professional learning conversation are ground rules.

Ground rules describe behaviors needed to have productive learning conversations. They keep participants honest to the process and the goal of the protocol. A school or team may adopt one set of ground rules to be used with any protocol. Ground rules are created to challenge a group to do its best learning together. A ground rule is added when a behavior is getting in the way of learning and removed when it no longer challenges the group. A protocol should allow time to reflect on the ground rules and make changes as needed.

It is best to have a limited number of ground rules. More than six may be too many for a group to remember. It is important to begin each learning conversation by revisiting the ground rules. A useful practice is laminating the ground rules and having the group facilitator distribute them at the beginning of the conversation and collect them at the end.

The following are some sample ground rules. Ground rules should be written as behaviors.

Figure 1.1

Ground Rules for Learning Conversations

1. Bring your most challenging, troublesome work to the conversation.

2. Celebrate feedback that challenges you to grow. (Praise is nice to hear, but does not help you improve.)

3. Listen deeply. Do not rehearse what you plan to say while others are speaking.

4. Help others feel comfortable when sharing their thoughts and challenges.

5. Be mindful of the protocol and keep the conversation focused.

6. Share the air, and invite silent members into the conversation.

Figure 1.2

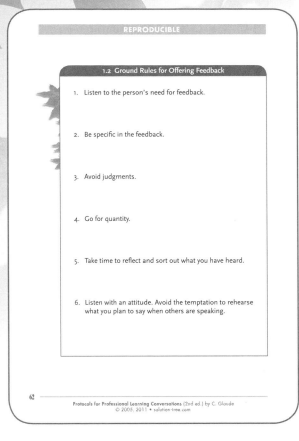

Ground Rules for Offering Feedback

Constructive feedback is an essential skill of learning conversations. The following ground rules may be helpful when offering feedback.

1. *Listen to the Person's Need for Feedback.* The most helpful feedback addresses the area of concern specified by the person presenting a challenge.

2. *Be Specific in the Feedback.* Feedback must be useful and understandable to the receiver. Offer concrete and specific descriptive feedback such as:

   • I noticed in the student work that student #1 was successful at reaching what you expected because I see [describe what you see in the work].

   • I feel that the models you gave students prior to this project were helpful because I see [describe what you see in the work].

   • I wonder if you considered doing [describe]during this assessment?

   • I can't tell if student #3 really has the concept because what I see in this work is [describe it].

   • I wonder if you had done [describe] would your results have been the same?

3. *Avoid Judgments.* The most helpful feedback describes what is seen or heard without labels such as "good" or "bad." Sometimes merely hearing others' perceptions about what they see in the student work will offer the educator valuable information. If the presenting educator asks you for advice, be clear to state it is your opinion.

4. *Go for Quantity.* The feedback you offer may be something that the presenter has already tried. Go for quantity when offering feedback so that the presenter will have many options to consider.

5. *Use a Protocol.* The protocols keep your limited time together focused. Remember the goal is to offer as much quality feedback as possible in a limited time. The protocol allows you to collect your thoughts and offer thoughtful feedback to your colleague.

6. *Listen With "an Attitude."* Even though you may not be presenting the challenge, insights from your colleagues may help you with your own challenges.

Ground Rules for Receiving Feedback

1. *Keep the spirit of improvement in mind.* Direct your colleagues to the areas where you want feedback. You will gain the most from this process if you present something current and challenging from your classroom work.

Figure 1.3

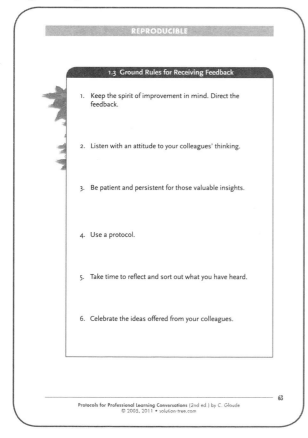

REPRODUCIBLE

1.3 Ground Rules for Receiving Feedback

1. Keep the spirit of improvement in mind. Direct the feedback.

2. Listen with an attitude to your colleagues' thinking.

3. Be patient and persistent for those valuable insights.

4. Use a protocol.

5. Take time to reflect and sort out what you have heard.

6. Celebrate the ideas offered from your colleagues.

63

Protocols for Professional Learning Conversations (2nd ed.) by C. Glaude
© 2005, 2011 • solution-tree.com

2. *Listen With an Attitude to Your Colleagues' Thinking.* Remember you are looking for new perspectives and ideas to improve your students' learning. Tune into differences in perspectives. Remaining silent when others offer you ideas and feedback may help you be open to feedback and resist the temptation to engage in conversation on only one topic.

3. *Be Patient and Persistent.* Some of the feedback offered to you will be ideas that you have already considered. Keep listening for those thoughts that may push you to consider something new or see something you did not see.

4. *Use a Protocol.* The protocols keep your limited time together focused. Remember the goal is to hear many ideas from all your colleagues. If you allow your conversation to wander or become focused on only one topic, you may lose some valuable insights from others.

5. *Take Time to Sort Out What You Have Heard.* Designate time in your meeting for considering the feedback offered and planning your next steps for improving learning.

6. *Celebrate Any Gifts From Your Colleagues.* Ideas, insights, and feedback that challenge you are the gifts your colleagues offer. Remember to give your colleagues feedback on their feedback. Tell them what you learned from them and how you plan to use it.

SECTION 2

Learning Conversations Focused on Common Text Readings

For a school or group with little experience in using protocols for focused learning conversations, text-based discussions are a place to begin. Even learning communities with advanced skills in working together may use these protocols to stimulate rich and focused discussions.

Text-based protocols are easy to create when the purpose of the discussion is clear. The following are some examples of protocols for text-based conversations. Most of these protocols are 30–60 minutes in length so they may be used during team or faculty meetings. The protocols may be adapted to fit the purpose of the learning discussion and the time constraints of the discussion. Bruce Wellman and Laura Lipton (2004) offer additional protocols for dialogues centered on text. Their protocols can be used for brief text readings and quick ten-minute discussions.

Discussion groups should be no larger than six members so all can contribute their thoughts. Group members should sit in a circle facing each other without tables in front of them. Note taking should not occur. Though it may feel unnatural at first, the procedure of having no table and not taking notes promotes deep listening to what others are saying. This sets the tone for how a group learns together.

2.1 Surfacing Significant Ideas

Purpose of the Protocol: To promote conversation around the main ideas of a text that have personal significance to the readers; to foster shared understanding of main ideas

Prior to the Conversation: Everyone reads the same text and highlights two passages that represent the most significant ideas. Everyone should be prepared to share these passages and say why they are significant to them. If the text is short, the group may choose to read it during the meeting.

(2 minutes) *Introduction.* A facilitator and timekeeper are designated. The ground rules and goal of the protocol are reviewed.

(1 minute) *Write the Quote or Passage.* Each person writes his/her short passages on a strip of chart paper and tapes these to the wall. There should be one passage on each strip of paper. (People should write large enough so all group members can read the writing. The page number of the text should be written beside the passage.)

(30 minutes) *Present the Significant Ideas.* One person begins by presenting one significant idea from the text, stating why it is significant and what implication it has for his or her work. Members of the group add to this idea after the presenter speaks. Each person has up to seven minutes to discuss the significant idea. This process is repeated until each person has presented a significant idea. If a significant idea is connected to another person's significant idea, the strips of chart paper should be moved close together. After everyone has discussed their idea and if time is available, the second set of significant ideas may be presented and discussed.

(3 minutes) *Closure.* The group summarizes what they have learned together. (If there are other small groups discussing the same text, these groups may report one insight to the larger group.)

(2 minutes) *Debrief the Process.* Group members comment briefly on how the Protocol supported their learning and how they might improve on it.

2.2 Challenging Assumptions

Purpose of the Protocol: To help build personal meaning and share understanding on one key concept from a text

(**2 minutes**) *Introduction.* Designate a facilitator and timekeeper. Review the ground rules and the purpose of the protocol.

(**13 minutes**) *Prior Knowledge.* Each person silently jots down thoughts about the meaning of the key concept by completing Column 1 on the graphic organizer in the appendix.

Read. Everyone reads the designated short passage in the text on this concept. As they finish reading, they may move any of their ideas from Column 1 to Column 2. They may also add to either column.

Figure 2.2

(**5 minutes**) *Partner Discussion.* Partners discuss the ideas on their graphic organizer. As they discuss, they may move any ideas from Column 1 to Column 2. They may also add to either column.

(**10 minutes**) *Expand the Discussion.* Each pair then joins another partner group to discuss the ideas on their graphic organizers.

REPRODUCIBLE

2.2 Challenging Assumptions

Column 1	Column 2
I think _____ is . . .	I think _____ is NOT . . .

64

Protocols for Professional Learning Conversations (2nd ed.) by C. Glaude
© 2005, 2011 • solution-tree.com

(5 minutes) *Summarize.* Together the two partner pairs create a group graphic organizer on chart paper outlining the ideas the group has about what this concept is and is not. (If there are many small groups, they may share these group charts with the larger group.)

(2 minutes) *Debrief the Process.* Participants briefly comment on how the protocol supported their learning and how the protocol might be improved.

Figure 2.3a

2.3 Supporting Evidence

Purpose of the Protocol: To support ideas with evidence from the text (rather than voicing opinions). The round-robin process encourages all voices to be heard.

Adapting This Protocol: This protocol is created for use with a passage from Richard Stiggins' book, *Student-Involved Classroom Assessment*. However, it may be adapted for any other common reading. It is best used with six to eight people in a group.

(2 minutes) *Introduction.* Designate a facilitator and timekeeper. Review the ground rules and the purpose of the protocol.

(8 minutes) *Silent Reading.* Read *Emily's Story: A Vision of Success* (pages 65–68), and complete the graphic organizer (page 69) in the appendix.

Figure 2.3b

| 2.3b Supporting Evidence ||
Key to Success	Evidence (page number)
Students understand their learning goals and what "meeting the standard" means.	Emily studied samples of writing to determine why they were good. (Page 9)

(8 minutes) *Key Concepts.* One person begins by writing one of his or her keys to success on chart paper and shares the evidence from the text and page number where the evidence was found. Do a round robin with each person commenting or adding to this key to success. Share personal experiences, beliefs, or insights about this key to success.

(24 minutes) *More Key Concepts.* Repeat the step above with the next person in the circle. Repeat until all keys to success have been charted.

(10 minutes) *Check With the Expert.* Silently read *Emily's Story: The Keys to Success* (pages 70–71) to determine what Richard Stiggins says are the keys to successful assessment in Emily's story. After reading, consider any differences in what your group discussed from what Stiggins says.

(2 minutes) *Debrief the Process.* Comment briefly on how the protocol supported your learning and how you might improve on the protocol.

Figure 2.3c

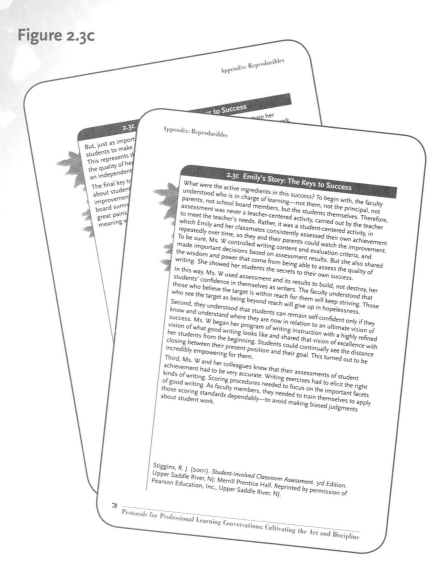

Appendix: Reproducibles

2.3c Emily's Story: The Keys to Success

What were the active ingredients in this success? To begin with, the faculty understood who is in charge of learning—not them, not the principal, not parents, not school board members, but the students themselves. Thus, assessment was never a teacher-centered activity, carried out by the teacher to meet the teacher's needs. Rather, it was a student-centered activity, in which Emily and her classmates consistently assessed their own achievement repeatedly over time, so they and their parents could watch the improvement.

To be sure, Ms. W controlled writing content and evaluation criteria, and made important decisions based on assessment results. But she also shared the wisdom and power that come from being able to assess the quality of writing. She showed her students the secrets to their own success.

In this way, Ms. W used assessment and its results to build, not destroy, her students' confidence in themselves as writers. The faculty understood that those who believe the target is within reach for them will keep striving. Those who see the target as being beyond reach will give up in hopelessness.

Second, they understood that students can remain self-confident only if they know and understand where they are now in relation to an ultimate vision of success. Ms. W began her program of writing instruction with a highly refined vision of what good writing looks like and shared that vision of excellence with her students from the beginning. Students could continually see the distance closing between their present position and their goal. This turned out to be incredibly empowering for them.

Third, Ms. W and her colleagues knew that their assessments of student achievement had to be very accurate. Writing exercises had to elicit the right kinds of writing. Scoring procedures needed to focus on the important facets of good writing. As faculty members, they needed to train themselves to apply those scoring standards dependably—to avoid making biased judgments about student work.

Stiggins, R. J. (2001). *Student-Involved Classroom Assessment.* 3rd Edition. Upper Saddle River, NJ: Merrill Prentice Hall. Reprinted by permission of Pearson Education, Inc., Upper Saddle River, NJ.

70 Protocols for Professional Learning Conversations: Cultivating the Art and Discipline

2.4 A Provocative Question

Purpose of the Protocol: To engage quick but thoughtful dialogue around provocative ideas based on current research; to prepare for a larger group conversation and future work around a common practice

Prior to the Conversation: A small group identifies or creates a policy statement focused on one practice that is important to this school. The policy statement must be grounded in current research. For example, it might be taken from the work of researchers such as Anne Davies (2000) on assessment practices, Ken O'Connor (1999) on grading, or Carol Ann Tomlinson (1999) on differentiating instruction.

(2 minutes) *Introduction.* Designate a group facilitator and timekeeper for the process. Review the ground rules and purpose of the protocol.

Figure 2.4

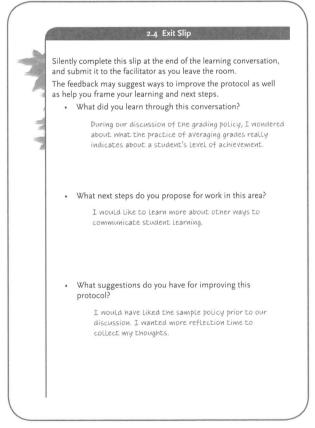

2.4 Exit Slip

Silently complete this slip at the end of the learning conversation, and submit it to the facilitator as you leave the room.

The feedback may suggest ways to improve the protocol as well as help you frame your learning and next steps.

- What did you learn through this conversation?

  During our discussion of the grading policy, I wondered about what the practice of averaging grades really indicates about a student's level of achievement.

- What next steps do you propose for work in this area?

  I would like to learn more about other ways to communicate student learning.

- What suggestions do you have for improving this protocol?

  I would have liked the sample policy prior to our discussion. I wanted more reflection time to collect my thoughts.

(4 minutes) *Read.* Silently read the proposed policy. Think how this policy would "fly" in your school or district.

(5 minutes) *Discuss With a Partner.* Discuss the implications of this policy with your partner. What do you think would fly? What do you think would not fly? What questions do you have about these policy statements? What intrigues you about it?

(8 minutes) *Expand the Conversation.* Join up with another partner group, and continue the conversation.

(3 minutes) *Personal Reflection.* Silently consider which statements from the policy would challenge your school or district to move forward in its development of this particular practice. If a policy in this area existed, what would you like to see in it?

(2 minutes) *Large-Group Closure.* In a larger group conversation, discuss any ideas around this policy that would challenge your school or district to move forward in its development of this practice.

(2 minutes) *Debrief the Process.* Silently write answers to the following questions and submit this "exit slip" to the facilitator as you leave the room. What did you learn through this conversation? What next steps do you propose for work in this area? What suggestions do you have for improving this protocol?

2.5 Text Rendering

Purpose of the Protocol: To collaboratively construct meaning; to clarify and to expand thinking about a reading

(2 minutes) *Introduction.* A facilitator for a larger group and a timekeeper are designated. The ground rules and purpose of the protocol are reviewed.

(15 minutes) *Key Ideas.* Each person reads a short selection and highlights one sentence, one phrase, and one word from the text that is personally significant. If the selection is a longer piece, this step may be completed prior to the conversation.

(6 minutes) *Key Sentences.* Each person shares a sentence from the reading, referencing the page number, and states why it seems significant. Members do not discuss the sentences, but listen for commonalities.

Key Phrases. Each person shares a phrase from the reading, referencing the page number, and states why he or she feels it is significant. Members do not discuss the phrases, but listen for commonalities.

Key Words. Each person shares a word from the reading that he or she feels is significant. The recorder charts these words on the white board or chart paper.

(30 minutes) *Discussion.* The group looks at the words charted and discusses what these words have to say about the reading.

(2 minutes) *Debrief the Process.* Group members comment briefly on how the protocol supported their learning and how they might improve on the protocol.

(5 minutes) *Closure.* One group insight is shared with the larger group.

Adapted from the National School Reform Faculty (2004).

2.6 The "Final Say" on Quotes

Purpose of the Protocol: To focus on evidence from the text; to expand personal meaning; to promote listening skills

Prior to the Conversation: A reading assignment is given, and individuals are asked to select three quotes from the selection that intrigue them and that they want to discuss with their colleagues.

(2 minutes) *Introduction.* A larger group facilitator and timekeeper are designated. The ground rules and purpose of the protocol are reviewed.

(5 minutes) *Preparation.* Each person silently reviews the text and prioritizes the three quotes to discuss with others.

(6 minutes each round) *Response to a Quote.* One person begins by citing the page number of one of his/her quotes and then reads the quote. The person reading the quote does not comment on it.

In round-robin style, moving around the circle, each person comments on the quote by offering thoughts or experiences or building on what was previously said. The person who presented the quote remains quiet during this exchange and listens for insights from others.

When the round robin is completed, the person who presented the quote has the final say and comments on the quote by stating the reason for its significance and what has been learned from colleagues about the quote.

New Rounds. After the first round is completed, the step above is repeated with a new person offering a quote. The rounds continue until there is no more time.

(2 minutes) *Debrief the Process.* Group members comment briefly on how the protocol supported their learning and how they might improve on the protocol.

Adapted from The Final Word Protocols (developed by Daniel Baron and Patricia Averette), which appear in McDonald, Mohr, Dichter, and McDonald, 2003, pp. 34–35.

2.7 Big Ideas Jigsaw

Purpose of the Protocol: To efficiently discuss a lengthy professional article during a faculty meeting or team time

Prior to the Conversation: The facilitator selects the article and draws a stop sign in the margin at about four places where he or she feels there should be discussion. Copies of the article are then made for all participants.

(2 minutes) *Introduction*. The facilitator sets the stage for why this article was selected and reviews the protocol. If there are four sections in the text, the participants are placed in groups of four.

(5 minutes) *Silent Reading*. Each person in the group is given a different section of the text to read. They are asked to prepare to present the key points or big ideas to their group members.

(12 minutes) *Presentation*. In order of the sections read, each person says something about the ideas in the text. After each person presents, clarifying questions may be asked. The group should be mindful of the time so that everyone has the opportunity to present ideas.

(10 minutes) *Discussion*. The small group explores any ideas that surfaced in the presentations.

(2 minutes) *Debrief/Exit Slip*. The facilitator may either do an oral debrief of what was learned from this discussion or he or she may have individuals complete an exit slip as they leave the meeting. A prompt on the exit slip might be: What was learned today, and what would you like us to further explore as a staff?

SECTION 3

Learning Conversations Focused on Personal Goals or Challenges

Educators set professional goals for improving their practice and improving the learning of their students. The following protocols may be useful to educators attempting to reflect on and refine the work toward their professional goals. Feedback from others helps individuals consider new options for improving their work toward professional challenges and goals.

Some of the protocols involve storytelling based on successful practices. Some involve storytelling based on challenging teaching incidences. Much can be learned from the collective experiences of colleagues. The storytelling protocols attempt to harvest this collective wisdom.

3.1 Refining a Professional Goal

Purpose of the Protocol: To help individuals refine their professional goals; to identify resources and support individuals may need as they work on their goals

(2 minutes) *Introduction.* Select a timekeeper and a facilitator. Review the purpose of the protocol and ground rules.

(3 minutes) *Presentation.* One person presents his or her professional improvement goal for the year using the frame found in Figure 3.1a. The group listens in silence.

(2 minutes) *Clarifying Questions.* Participants ask clarifying questions about the proposed goal to help them fully understand it. Clarifying questions involve yes or no answers. If a discussion begins to evolve, the facilitator should redirect the group to ask only clarifying questions.

Figure 3.1a

(10 minutes) *Playback.* Colleagues discuss what they heard about the presenter's goal using the frame found in Figure 3.1b. The presenter is silent as colleagues speak.

(8 minutes) *Follow-up.* The presenter may follow-up or comment on any issue raised during the playback session.

Figure 3.1b

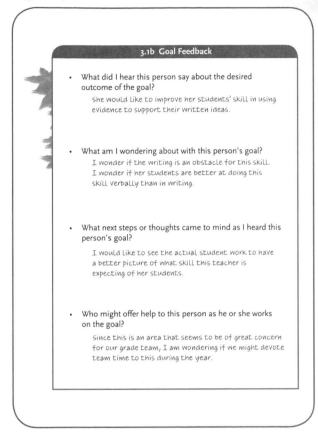

3.1b Goal Feedback

- What did I hear this person say about the desired outcome of the goal?

  She would like to improve her students' skill in using evidence to support their written ideas.

- What am I wondering about with this person's goal?

  I wonder if the writing is an obstacle for this skill. I wonder if her students are better at doing this skill verbally than in writing.

- What next steps or thoughts came to mind as I heard this person's goal?

  I would like to see the actual student work to have a better picture of what skill this teacher is expecting of her students.

- Who might offer help to this person as he or she works on the goal?

  Since this is an area that seems to be of great concern for our grade team, I am wondering if we might devote team time to this during the year.

(2 minutes) *Debrief the Process.* Group members comment briefly on how the protocol supported their learning and how they might improve on the protocol.

(5 minutes) *Reflection.* The presenter silently writes any ideas for refining the goal or plan or for working on the goal.

3.2 Feedback on Personal Work Toward a Professional Goal

Purpose of the Protocol: To receive feedback on a teaching practice that is forwarding a personal goal

Prior to the Conversation: The presenting educator selects some aspect of his/her work completed toward a professional goal about which he or she wants feedback. Copies of any materials of this work should be made for each member of the group. It is best to have small groups of four or five. If student work is shared, the names must be removed and each student work sample replaced with a number or letter. Removing names protects confidentiality and removes bias.

(2 minutes) *Getting Started.* Select a facilitator, a timekeeper, and a recorder. Review the purpose of the protocol and ground rules for this process.

(4 minutes) *Directing Feedback.* The presenting educator describes the work and how it connects to a professional goal. He or she explains any context or background to help others understand this work and describes what particular part of the work seems challenging. This challenge should direct the participants' feedback. Participants remain silent during this presentation.

(4 minutes) *Clarifying Questions.* Participants ask clarifying questions about the work and the challenge to help them fully understand it. Clarifying questions involve yes or no answers. If a discussion begins to evolve, the facilitator should redirect the group to ask clarifying questions.

(2 minutes) *Collecting Thoughts.* Participants silently prepare their feedback. The ground rules for giving feedback found in Section 1 may be helpful.

(20 minutes) *Feedback.* The participants brainstorm ideas and offer feedback related to the challenge area. The presenting educator is silent during this exchange. The recorder takes notes on the feedback offered for the presenting educator so he or she may reflect on the ideas at a later time.

(10 minutes) *Conversation.* The presenting educator invites the participants into a conversation to explore any of the feedback or ideas offered. The presenting educator directs the conversation. Only one or two ideas may be explored.

(3 minutes) *Debrief.* In round-robin style, moving quickly around the circle, everyone gives a quick response to the following: What did we learn? How might we improve this protocol?

3.3 Storytelling About Personal Teaching Challenges

Purpose of the Protocol: To receive feedback from others on teaching challenges

Prior to the Conversation: Each educator should select an area of challenge to bring to the group. An individual should consider the following as he or she selects the area of challenge: What really challenges me in my work with students? This should be something the teacher wants to improve and desires feedback from others. This may be:

- a professional improvement goal
- an especially challenging skill or concept for students
- an assessment or instructional strategy that has not worked as hoped
- a classroom management issue

The presenting teacher should be specific about what he or she wants to improve.

(2 minutes)   *Getting Started.* Select a facilitator, a timekeeper, and a recorder. Review the purpose of the protocol and ground rules for this process.

(2 minutes)   *Present the Challenge.* One person begins by telling her or his challenge to the group. What specifically would you like to improve and why did you select this? What have you already done to work on this challenge?

(6 minutes)   *Interview.* Group members interview the person with the challenge to help the individual describe the challenge in more detail. They ask probing questions. Questions should be challenging, but not threatening.

(5 minutes each round)   *Wonderings. Round 1.* Group members offer specific "I wonder . . ." questions (for example, I wonder if doing exit slips at the end of the class might help you pre-assess where your students are on this skill?). The educator presenting the challenge remains silent and does not respond to the "I wonder" questions. The recorder takes notes about the "I wonders" offered so the person presenting can listen actively to the ideas.
Round 2. Another person in the group repeats the above steps with his or her challenge. If time permits, a round may be repeated for each person in the group.

(2 minutes)   *Debrief the Process.* Group members comment briefly on how the protocol supported their learning and how they might improve upon the protocol.

(5 minutes)   *Action Plan Reflection.* Each person reads the "I wonder" notes and reflects on his or her next steps for addressing the challenge.

3.4 Feedback on a Teaching Conundrum

Purpose of the Protocol: To learn from a challenge which occurred during teaching

Prior to the Conversation: The presenting educator considers one teaching challenge about which she or he desires feedback. The presenting teacher then frames the challenging situation by writing the scenario in five to seven sentences. Copies of the written scenario are made for each group member. By describing the challenge in writing prior to the conversation, the presenting teacher is encouraged to capture the essence of the challenge. In addition, the written description focuses feedback and allows colleagues to comment on key phrases and words the writer used.

(2 minutes) *Getting Started.* Select a facilitator and a timekeeper. Review the purpose of the protocol and ground rules for this process.

(4 minutes) *Reflection on the Conundrum.* Colleagues read the scenario in silence. They take a few minutes to collect their thoughts about the challenge.

(10 minutes) *Feedback.* Colleagues discuss the challenging scenario by offering insights they have on the conundrum, commenting on the words or phrases the presenting teacher used, raising questions, or offering steps to take. The presenter does not engage in conversation, but takes notes on anything of interest during the discussion. Since the presenter may have already considered some of the feedback and ideas, he or she listens for any nuggets of information that may be helpful.

(4 minutes) *Conversation.* The presenter invites the participants into a conversation to explore any of the feedback or ideas offered. Probably only one idea may be explored.

(2 minutes) *Debrief the Process.* Group members briefly comment on how the protocol supported their learning and how they might improve on the protocol.

(5 minutes) *Personal Reflection.* The presenting teacher reads the notes from the session, records what he or she learned from sharing this incident, and lists any next steps.

3.5 Learning From Success Stories

Purpose of the Protocol: To learn from the successes of colleagues who faced a particular challenge

Prior to the Conversation: The group members are given a focus for their inquiry. Examples of inquiry focus areas are:

- Recall a time when you successfully helped your students understand and own the expectations for high-quality work.
- Think of a success story you have had with a student who was struggling in your class.

Each group member considers the focus and prepares what he or she will share with the group. This is best done with groups of six people.

(2 minutes) *Getting Started.* Select a facilitator and a timekeeper. Review the purpose of the protocol and ground rules for this process. The focus statement is written on the board or on chart paper.

(40 minutes) *Storytelling.* In round-robin style, moving around the circle, each person tells his or her story without interruption for up to five minutes.

Question and Answer. After each person tells his or her story, people may ask questions for two to three minutes. The timekeeper keeps the process moving.

(5 minutes) *Learnings Debriefed.* In round-robin style, moving quickly around the circle, each person says one thing he or she learned from these stories. If there is a larger group, each small group may report out their learning.

3.6 Offering a Best Practice

Purpose of the Protocol: To learn from a colleague's successful practice

Prior to the Conversation: Each person prepares to present a successful practice and to state the reason he or she believes the practice worked. Copies of materials from the practice should be made for each member of the group. If student work is shared, the names must be removed and replaced with numbers or letters.

(2 minutes)   *Getting Started.* Select a facilitator and a timekeeper. Review the purpose of the protocol and ground rules for this process.

(8 minutes)   *Background.* One person describes the successful practice, explaining the context of the practice, how students responded or performed (student work may be displayed), and why he or she believes it was successful. Participants remain silent.

(4 minutes)   *Clarifying Questions.* Participants ask clarifying questions about the work and the challenge to help them fully understand it. Clarifying questions involve yes or no answers. If a discussion begins to evolve, the facilitator should redirect the group to ask clarifying questions.

(3 minutes)   *Reflection.* Everyone reflects on the presentation and thinks of questions about the practice. Each person prepares to engage in a conversation about the practice.

(20 minutes) *Conversation.* Everyone participates in a conversation about the practice. Questions posed by the participants or presenter might be:

- What are the presenter's next steps in this practice?
- How might it be modified for other content areas?
- What did we learn from this practice?
- What do we notice in the materials or student work presented?

(10 minutes) *Learning.* In round-robin style, moving around the circle, each person has the opportunity to name what they learned from this practice, OR an idea they want to pursue, OR a question they have about the practice.

(2 minutes)   *Debrief the Process.* Group members comment briefly on how the protocol supported their learning and how they might improve on the protocol.

3.7 Refining a Unit Plan

Purpose of the Protocol: To gather feedback to strengthen a unit plan

Prior to the Conversation: The person presenting a unit plan completes the Unit Plan Guide (see Figure 3.7) and brings copies of these responses to the session.

(2 minutes) *Getting Started.* Select a facilitator, a recorder, and a timekeeper. Review the purpose of the protocol and ground rules for this process.

(8 minutes) *Background.* The presenting teacher talks through the Unit Plan Guide, emphasizing any areas in which he or she especially desires feedback. Each person is given a blank Unit Plan Guide for note-taking as the teacher presents ideas.

Figure 3.7

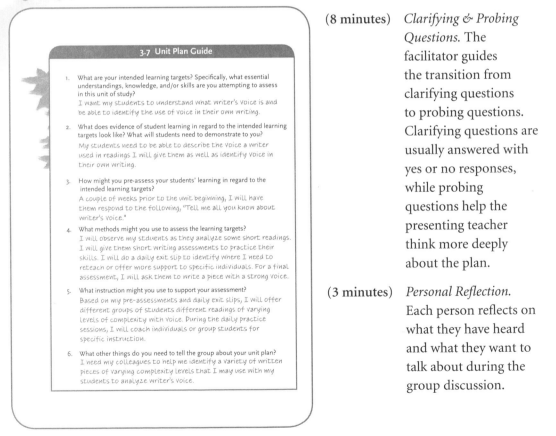

(8 minutes) *Clarifying & Probing Questions.* The facilitator guides the transition from clarifying questions to probing questions. Clarifying questions are usually answered with yes or no responses, while probing questions help the presenting teacher think more deeply about the plan.

(3 minutes) *Personal Reflection.* Each person reflects on what they have heard and what they want to talk about during the group discussion.

(8 minutes)   *Group Discussion.* The group pays extra attention to the areas the presenters emphasized during the presentation part of the protocol. The facilitator records ideas on a blank Unit Plan Guide. The presenting teacher is silent.

(10 minutes)   *Open Discussion.* The presenting teacher responds freely and invites group members into an open discussion about any of the ideas.

(2 minutes)   *Debrief the Process.* Group members comment briefly on how the protocol supported their learning and how they might improve on the protocol. Notes from the conversation are given to the presenting teacher to reflect on at a later time.

SECTION 4

Learning Conversations Focused on Student Work

L ooking at student work has long been an individual teacher's task; something often done in the evening and in isolation from colleagues. Yet student work should be the centerpiece of collaborative discussions about improving teaching and learning. Student work can be the context of some of the most meaningful and powerful professional development opportunities. As with all protocols, adapt these to fit the purpose of the collaborative inquiry and to match time constraints.

4.1 Do You See What I See?

Purpose of the Protocol: To learn from what others see in the student work. By listening fully to what others see in the student work, a teacher may gain information about both the learning and the teaching. This protocol may be used to address the question of validity of an assessment or an assignment by answering, "Does this assessment really assess what it intends to assess?"

Prior to the Conversation: The presenting teacher needs to select three samples of student work that represent a range of quality responses to the assignment or assessment. For confidentiality and to remove bias, student names are removed and the work is labeled Student A, Student B, and Student C. Copies of student work samples are made for everyone in the group.

Figure 4.1

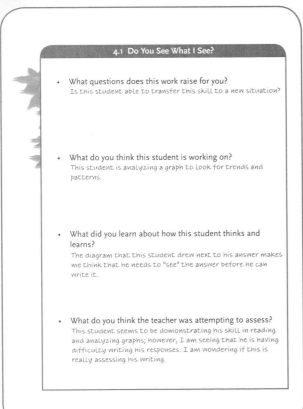

4.1 Do You See What I See?

- What questions does this work raise for you?
  Is this student able to transfer this skill to a new situation?

- What do you think this student is working on?
  This student is analyzing a graph to look for trends and patterns.

- What did you learn about how this student thinks and learns?
  The diagram that this student drew next to his answer makes me think that he needs to "see" the answer before he can write it.

- What do you think the teacher was attempting to assess?
  This student seems to be demonstrating his skill in reading and analyzing graphs; however, I am seeing that he is having difficulty writing his responses. I am wondering if this is really assessing his writing.

(**2 minutes**) *Getting Started.* Select a facilitator and a timekeeper. Review the purpose of the protocol and ground rules for this process.

(**8 minutes**) *Silent Reflection.* The presenting teacher distributes the student work. Nothing is said about the work, its context, or the students. The participants scan the work in silence, making notes about what they see in the learning (see Figure 4.1).

(8 minutes) *Describing the Work.* The facilitator asks, "What did you see in the work?" Participants respond without judgment about the quality of the work and the evidence of learning that they see. If judgments emerge, the facilitator reminds the speaker to describe the evidence on which the judgment was made. The presenting teacher remains quiet and takes notes.

(8 minutes) *Raising Questions and Hunches.* The facilitator asks:

- What questions does this work raise for you?
- What do you think this student is working on?
- What did you learn about how this student thinks and learns?
- What do you think the teacher was attempting to assess?

Group members offer their questions and ideas. The presenting teacher remains quiet and takes notes.

(15 minutes) *Dialogue.* At the facilitator's invitation, the presenting teacher responds to anything learned from colleagues or any questions he or she wants to pursue. The facilitator asks:

- What new perspectives did you learn about student learning from your colleagues?
- What questions were raised that you may wish to pursue to improve the learning?
- Are there new ideas that you might like to try in your classroom?

The presenting teacher invites other colleagues into the discussion.

(5 minutes) *Reflection on the Conversation.* The group discusses how they experienced this conference and what they learned.

Adapted from the Collaborative Assessment Conference Protocol by the Coalition of Essential Schools. Box 1969, Brown University, Providence, RI 02912. www.essentialschools.org

4.2 What Is the Goal?

Purpose of the Protocol: To analyze whether a particular assessment method was a match for the intended learning outcome

Prior to the Conversation: The presenting teacher selects three samples of student work that represent a range of quality responses to the assignment or assessment. For confidentiality and to remove bias, student names are removed and the work is labeled Student A, Student B, and Student C. Copies of the samples are made for everyone in the group or enlarged so all can view them. Sometimes it is helpful to photograph student samples and display them using an LCD projector.

(2 minutes) *Getting Started.* Select a facilitator and a timekeeper. Review the purpose of the protocol and ground rules for this process.

Figure 4.2

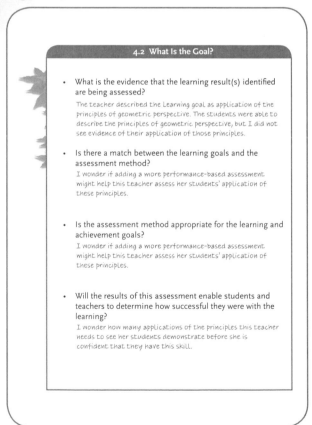

(4 minutes) *Learning Outcomes.* The presenting teacher outlines what learning goals are being assessed, the context of the assessment, and how the assessment was conducted.

(4 minutes) *Review of the Work.* Colleagues view the student work and make notes (see Figure 4.2), reflecting on the following:

- What is the evidence that the learning result(s) identified are being assessed?

- Is there a match between the learning goals and the assessment method?

- Is the assessment method appropriate for the learning and achievement goals?

- Will the results of this assessment enable students and teachers to determine how successful they were with the learning?

(8 minutes) *Feedback Offered.* The group members offer their feedback to the questions above while the presenting teacher is silent.

(3 minutes) *Exploration.* The presenting teacher invites colleagues into a conversation to explore any issues offered.

(5 minutes) *Reflection on the Conversation.* The group discusses how they experienced this conversation and what they learned.

4.3 Refining the Rubric

Purpose of the Protocol: To refine a rubric by considering the different levels of quality in the student work

Prior to the Conversation: The presenting teacher selects four to five samples of student work that represent a range of quality. For confidentiality and to remove bias, student names are removed and the work is labeled Student A, Student B, and Student C. Copies of each of the work samples, along with the rubric, are made for everyone in the group.

(2 minutes)   *Getting Started.* Select a facilitator and a timekeeper. Review the purpose of the protocol and ground rules for this process.

(2 minutes)   *Learning Goal.* The presenting teacher describes the learning goals being assessed.

(4 minutes)   *Review.* The group looks silently at the student work and considers the following: When you look at the student work, does the rubric reflect the most tangible and appropriate differences in quality? Why or why not? What would you change about this rubric?

(5 minutes)   *Feedback.* Group members discuss their insights to the questions above while the presenting teacher is quiet and takes notes.

(8 minutes)   *Feedback on the Feedback.* The presenting teacher explores any ideas offered during the feedback.

(5 minutes)   *Reflection on the Conversation.* The group discusses how they experienced this conversation and what they learned.

4.4 Focused Feedback

Purpose of the Protocol: To focus the feedback a presenting teacher desires from the group

Prior to the Conversation: The presenting teacher identifies a focus question for his or her feedback session (for example, Would you agree that this is high-quality work for this grade level?). For confidentiality and to remove bias, student names are removed, and student work is labeled Student A, Student B, and Student C. Copies of the work are made for everyone in the group. If student work is lengthy, the work and the focus question may be given ahead of time.

(2 minutes) *Getting Started.* Select a facilitator and a timekeeper. Review the purpose of the protocol and ground rules for this process.

(5 minutes) *Context.* The presenting teacher offers any background information and the purpose for the assessment. The focus question is written on chart paper or the board for all to see.

(5 minutes) *Review.* The group members review the student work in regard to the focus question.

(8 minutes) *Group Discussion.* Using the focus question as their guide, group members generate their insights and observations by what they see in the work. The presenting teacher is quiet.

(5 minutes) *Dialogue.* The presenting teacher joins the discussion and directs conversation to any intriguing ideas or points to pursue.

(5 minutes) *Reflection on the Conversation.* The group discusses how they experienced this conversation and what they learned.

4.5 A Cross Section of Student Work Focused on a Specific Learning Goal

Purpose of the Protocol: To reflect on what seems evident about student learning by studying a cross section of student work focused on a particular learning goal. There is no presenter for this session. This cross section of work may be small or large; the session may be done at a grade level or school level. It is intended that the session not become bogged down in assumptions and evaluations.

Prior to the Conversation: The group identifies a learning goal for the focus of their session (for example, grade 5 students' abilities to weave evidence into their writing to support their answers). Each person in the group collects several examples of student work that demonstrates this focus. For confidentiality and to remove bias, student names are removed, and student work is labeled Student A, Student B, and Student C. Copies of the work are made for everyone in the group.

(2 minutes) *Getting Started.* Select a facilitator and a timekeeper. Review the purpose of the protocol and ground rules for this process. Student work is labeled and names are removed. The teacher writes the learning goal on chart paper or the board so colleagues can keep it as the focus as they study the student work.

(5 minutes) *Study.* The student work is distributed, and individuals consider the focus by addressing the following:

- What did you see in the work that demonstrates this learning goal?
- What was interesting or surprising?
- What questions does this student work raise?

(4 minutes) *Discussion.* The members of the group discuss their thoughts about the questions above. The facilitator reminds the group to point to the evidence in the student work as they discuss their ideas.

(3 minutes) *Next Steps.* The group debriefs what they learned from today's inquiry and any next steps they want to take as a team or school.

Adapted from the Slice Protocol by the Coalition of Essential Schools. Box 1969, Brown University, Providence, RI 02912. www.essentialschools.org

4.6 Fishbowl Seminar

Purpose of the Protocol: To have colleagues offer reflections about the work of students they do not know

Prior to the Conversation: Two grade-level teams identify one area of student learning they would like to explore (for example, expository writing). Each grade-level team selects several samples of student work to share. For confidentiality and to remove bias, student names are removed, and the work is labeled Student A, Student B, and Student C. Copies of the student work are made for each member of the group.

(2 minutes) *Getting Started.* Select a facilitator and a timekeeper. Review the purpose of the protocol and ground rules for this process. Student work is exchanged between the grade-level teams. For example, grades 5 and 6 teachers trade copies of work by their students. If the work is lengthy, it may be read prior to this session.

(4 minutes) *Reflection.* The work offered is reviewed by the other grade-level team using Fishbowl Feedback Guidelines.

Figure 4.6

Fishbowl Feedback Guidelines

- Stay focused on the evidence that you see in the student's work.
- Avoid judging what you see; merely describe what you see.
- Look openly and broadly; don't let your expectations cloud your views.
- Listen without judgment to what others are saying.
- Focus on understanding different points of view.
- Do not offer background information to various assignments; let the student work speak for itself.

(35 minutes) *Fishbowl Discussion. Round 1.* Participants sit in fishbowl style with the presenting team sitting in the outer circle and the team offering feedback sitting in the inner circle. The facilitator leads the seminar. The student work is the "text" of the seminar. The grade-level team that offered the work silently observes this fishbowl discussion as the team in the inner circle discusses what they see in the work, raises questions, and offers insights.

(35 minutes) *Round 2.* The teams switch places, and the process is repeated with the other team discussing the work of the preceding team.

(15 minutes) *Debrief.* The facilitator asks both teams, "What have we learned of value about improving student learning in this area and why?"

4.7 Making a Commitment to Improve the Learning

Purpose of the Protocol: To analyze the results of a common assessment and to design a plan for improving the learning. This protocol is intended for teachers who work together with the same group of students.

Prior to the Conversation: The results of a common assessment are collected. Copies of representative student work are prepared by removing the names and labeling the work. Any numerical data from assessment scores is merely presented with no written summary findings.

(2 minutes) *Getting Started.* Select a facilitator and a timekeeper. Review the purpose of the protocol, the ground rules for this process, and the skills or concepts assessed.

(2 minutes) *Predicting the Results.* Before the team analyzes the results from the assessment, they predict how they think their students did by silently reflecting on the following questions:

- Where do you think students scored highest?
- Where do you think students scored lowest?
- What are your assumptions behind your predictions?
- Why did you make these predictions?

(6 minutes) *Discussing Predictions and Assumptions.* Each group member shares his or her predictions and the assumption behind each prediction. This helps members uncover their biases and prepare for a full inspection of the data.

(10 minutes) *Data Analysis.* The group compares their predictions to the actual results of the assessment. As a group, they identify areas in learning that they would like to improve.

(20 minutes) *A Commitment.* The group selects one area, indicated from the assessment results, that they are passionate about improving. Together they generate a team plan for what they will do with students, how they will keep this discussion alive during future team meetings, and how they will collect data to see if their efforts are making a difference. This may become a collaborative action research plan for this team for this year.

SECTION 5

Learning Conversations Focused on Action Research to Improve Student Learning

Great teachers engage daily in action research. They learn new ways to improve their instruction and assessments, they implement strategies, reflect on the results of student learning, and continuously improve their practices. Yet action research becomes even more powerful when the collective expertise and knowledge of a group of professionals is offered to an individual's inquiry. Learning conversations may occur as an individual is refining his or her area of action research, planning a research strategy, or analyzing the student data.

5.1 Narrowing the Inquiry Focus

Purpose of the Protocol: To help an individual to get in touch with the core issues of practice that matter most to him or her

Prior to the Conversation: Review the Action Research Cycle (see Figure 5.1), and identify possible areas for research. One person volunteers to discuss a general area for action research. This person desires to narrow his or her inquiry and needs the assistance of others to focus the study.

(3 minutes) *Getting Started.* Choose a facilitator and a time keeper. Review the purpose of the protocol and ground rules.

(21 minutes) *Reflective Interview.* One person volunteers to be interviewed by the other members of the group. The interviewers only ask clarifying and probing questions about the area of action research that the person is considering. The following are guidelines for the interview:

- Make the interview challenging, but not threatening.
- Try to elicit responses of depth and breadth.
- Do not engage in discussion of any other topics.

Figure 5.1

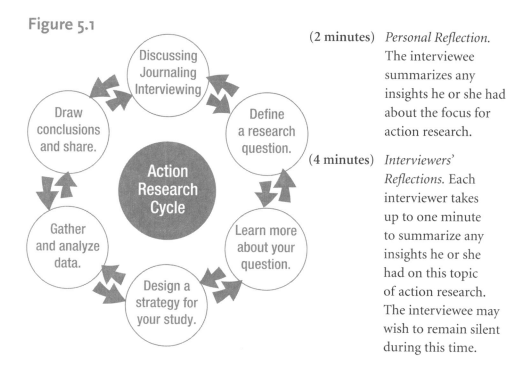

(2 minutes) *Personal Reflection.* The interviewee summarizes any insights he or she had about the focus for action research.

(4 minutes) *Interviewers' Reflections.* Each interviewer takes up to one minute to summarize any insights he or she had on this topic of action research. The interviewee may wish to remain silent during this time.

5.2 Refining the Inquiry Question

Purpose of the Protocol: To give feedback to an individual who has a clear idea about the question he or she wants to research

(3 minutes) *Getting Started.* Choose a facilitator and a timekeeper. Review the purpose of the protocol and relevant ground rules.

(2 minutes) *Presentation of the Area of Focus.* One person shares the question he or she has chosen for action research. Write this question on the chart paper or board for others. Colleagues are silent and take notes as the presenter addresses the following questions:

Figure 5.2a

- Who will this research affect?
- Why is it important to me?
- What do I want to improve?
- What do I suspect is causing the problem?
- What type of a problem is it?
- What am I proposing to do about it?
- What would I hope to see at the end of my research?

Figure 5.2b

Criteria for a High-Quality Action Research Question
• Looks at improving student learning • Is something a teacher can influence • Is something a teacher is deeply concerned about • Is possible with a narrow focus

(19 minutes)   *Analytical Discourse.* Members of the group repeat back what they have heard from the presenter. They ask clarifying and probing questions to help the presenter fully describe the research challenge. They consider the Criteria for a High-Quality Action Research Question as they offer their interpretations (see Figure 5.2b).

(2 minutes)   *Suggested Questions.* Do a round robin with any person offering a modified research question suggestion. No discussions occur at this time. It may be helpful to write the question on a slip of paper.

(2 minutes)   *Personal Reflection.* The presenter offers any insights he or she has about the action research question.

5.3 Feedback on Data Collection Strategies

Purpose of the Protocol: To assist an individual who has a research question and needs feedback on ways to collect data

(2 minutes) *Getting Started.* Choose a facilitator and a timekeeper. Review the purpose of the protocol and ground rules for the process.

(2 minutes) *Presentation of the Question.* The individual shares his or her action research question, writes it on a white board or chart paper, and explains what results he or she hopes will result from this study.

(3 minutes) *Clarifying Questions.* Group members ask clarifying questions about the research question. They do not discuss the topic.

(15 minutes) *Discussion of Data Collection Methods.* Group members offer their ideas about how they might collect data on this research question. This is an open brainstorming session. Do not get hung up discussing one method. Go for quantity. The person with the question remains silent and takes notes.

(9 minutes) *General Discussion.* The person with the question follows up on any data collection suggestions by asking more questions of the group.

(2 minutes) *Personal Reflection.* The person with the question offers any insights about his or her learning.

5.4 Feedback on Data Collection Plan

Purpose of the Protocol: To assist an individual in creating a plan for collecting data for a chosen research question

(2 minutes) *Getting Started.* Choose a facilitator and a timekeeper. Review the purpose of the protocol and relevant ground rules.

(2 minutes) *Presentation of the Question.* The individual shares his or her action research question, writes it on a white board or chart paper, and explains what results he or she hopes will result from this study.

(2 minutes) *Reflect Back.* Group members reflect back what they heard about the plan for collecting data. They do not discuss or offer feedback at this time. The presenter is silent.

(2 minutes) *Response.* The presenter briefly responds to others' expressed understanding of the research and data collection process and provides further clarification if needed.

(8 minutes) *Brainstorming Methods.* Group members offer their ideas about how they might collect data on this research question. This is an open brainstorming session. Do not get hung up discussing one method. Go for quantity. The person presenting remains silent and takes notes.

(8 minutes) *General Discussion.* The presenter follows up on any data collection suggestions by asking more questions of the group.

(2 minutes) *Personal Reflection.* The presenter offers any insights about his or her learning.

5.5 Feedback on Student Data Collected

Purpose of the Protocol: To assist an individual who has implemented a strategy or strategies during the study and has collected some data

(2 minutes) *Getting Started.* Choose a facilitator and a timekeeper. Review the purpose of the protocol and relevant ground rules.

(4 minutes) *Presentation of the Data.* One person shares the question he or she has chosen for action research. Write this question for others. He or she then describes the strategy used and shares the data. Data might be qualitative or quantitative. It may be in digital (for example, electronic, video, audio, multimedia) or print form. Copies of any information or data should be made in advance for everyone. Remember to remove student names from all of the work. The presenter may describe impressions of what the data says or how he or she perceived the strategy working and may direct the group to any areas where feedback is needed.

(2 minutes) *Reflection.* Group members review the data and prepare responses.

(5 minutes) *Raising Questions.* Group members discuss questions, insights, or feedback that the use of the strategy/strategies raised for them. The presenter is silent and takes notes on any areas that he or she may wish to discuss later.

(13 minutes) *Conversation.* The presenter directs a conversation on any questions, insights, or feedback offered.

(2 minutes) *Personal Reflection.* The presenter offers any insights about his or her learning and names possible next steps.

5.6 Feedback on What Was Learned From the Study

Purpose of the Protocol: To offer feedback on the conclusions an individual has made from the action research study

Prior to the Conversation: The presenter organizes the data analyzed from the action research study and prepares to offer any conclusions from this study. Copies of any information or data should be made in advance for all group members. Please remember to remove any student names from all of the work. Data may be presented in a variety of forms—print, audio, video, electronic, multimedia, or digital.

(2 minutes) *Getting Started.* Choose a facilitator and a timekeeper. Review the purpose of the protocol and relevant ground rules.

(8 minutes) *Presentation of the Data.* One person shares the question he or she has chosen for action research. Write this question on a white board for others. The presenting teacher then shares the data collected and his or her impressions about the data and responds to the following questions:

- What was learned from the data?
- What impact do the data have on learning and on future teaching practice?
- Were there any surprises?
- What are the next steps or future questions?

(2 minutes) *Reflection.* Group members take a moment to prepare their responses.

(10 minutes) *Raising Questions.* In round-robin style, group members share the questions they have about the findings of this study. The presenting teacher is silent.

(10 minutes) *Conversation.* The presenter directs a conversation on any questions, insights, or feedback that surfaced while questions were raised.

(2 minutes) *Personal Reflection.* The presenter offers any insights about his or her learning and any next steps he or she will take.

5.7 Generating Potential Future Research Questions

Purpose of the Protocol: To brainstorm possible future action research questions resulting from a current action research. This protocol is to be used after an action research study is concluded.

(2 minutes) *Getting Started.* Choose a facilitator and a timekeeper. Review the purpose of the protocol and relevant ground rules.

(10 minutes) *Interviewing.* The teacher who has completed an action research is interviewed by a group of colleagues. They ask probing questions and clarifying questions such as:

- What was learned from the study?
- Were there any surprises?
- What questions were left unanswered?
- What is the teacher still wondering about?

The group does not engage in discussion at this time.

(5 minutes) *Paraphrase.* The presenting teacher listens silently as the group paraphrases what they learned from the interview session. They also comment on ideas in which they noticed the teacher showed special interest. By hearing the story played back in this fashion, the teacher may have insights into next steps for the study.

(5 minutes) *Discussion.* The presenter directs a conversation about any possible future research questions generated during this session.

(2 minutes) *Personal Reflection.* The presenter offers any insights about his or her learning and any next steps he or she will take. This may be accomplished in writing.

SECTION 6

Other Applications for Protocols

The suggested protocols outlined in this book are merely a starting point. As groups and facilitators become more skillful with professional learning conversations, they will begin to create their own protocols. The following questions may guide the development or adaptation of protocols:

- What is the purpose for the protocol? What learning do we need to do together?
- How much time is available for the learning conversation?
- Who will join the conversation? Are there existing group behaviors where ground rules may be useful?
- Are there any protocols that we might adapt?
- How do we prepare participants for the protocol?

Protocols are also powerful tools for work with students. The text-based protocols in Section 2 of this book may be used or adapted for discussions with students. The protocols guide thoughtful classroom discussions by requiring that students identify key ideas and support their answers with evidence from the text. The protocols help students make meaning of a text while modeling good comprehension skills.

Peer critique is a powerful way to involve students in the assessment process. The protocols in Section 4 focus on involving collegial feedback on individual work and may be adapted and used when students bring their work for peer feedback.

In summary, a skillful educator may create or adapt protocols to promote and navigate both collegial and classroom learning. Some protocols work best with some groups while others must be adapted to suit the needs. Like good teaching, using a protocol to foster conversation is both an art and a discipline.

Acknowledgments

I want to acknowledge the fine work of the Coalition of Essential Schools. Their website for looking at student work and their resources for Critical Friends Groups have given me exemplars and a template to create my own protocols.

Bruce Wellman's work on data-driven dialogues has inspired me to create ways for educators to talk together and make meaning of all kinds of data in support of our students' learning and our school system's improvement.

Richard Sagor's book *How to Conduct Collaborative Action Research* prompted me to create conversations that would support my colleagues' learning through research in their own classroom and schools.

I would like to thank Anne Davies for her work on classroom assessment. Our conversations and work together have resulted in protocols that help educators focus on what really matters—children and their learning.

My colleagues, Melissa Noack and Jane Golding, helped to create graphics representing complex ideas that arose from our work together in simple ways. The graphics and our rich conversations support my ongoing learning and influenced the design of this book. Their generosity and the support of my colleagues helped it find its way to creation.

References

Coalition of Essential Schools. Box 1969, Brown University, Providence, RI, 02912. www.essentialschools.org

Davies, A. (2000). *Making Classroom Assessment Work*. Courtenay, BC: Connections Publishing.

Johnson, S. M. (1990). *Teachers at Work: Achieving Success in Our Schools*. New York: Basic Books.

McDonald, J. P., Mohr, N., Dichter, A., and McDonald, E. C. (2003). *The Power of Protocols: An Educator's Guide to Better Practice*. New York: Teachers College Press.

National School Reform Faculty. (2004). Bloomington, IN. www.nsrfharmony.org

O'Connor, K. (1999). *How to Grade for Learning*. Arlington Heights, IL: Skylight Training.

Sagor, R. (1992). *How to Conduct Collaborative Research*. Alexandria, VA: ASCD.

Stiggins, R. J. (2001). *Student-Involved Classroom Assessment*. 3rd Edition. Upper Saddle River, NJ: Merrill Prentice Hall.

Tomlinson, C. (1999) *The Differentiated Classroom: Responding to the Needs of All Learners*. Alexandria, VA: ASCD.

Wellman, B. and Lipton, L. (2004). *Data-Driven Dialogue*. Sherman, CT: MiraVia.

Appendix: Reproducibles

Note: The following pages may be reproduced for learning conversations only.

1.1 Ground Rules for Learning Conversations

1. Bring your most challenging, troublesome work to the conversation.

2. Celebrate feedback that challenges you to grow. (Praise is nice to hear but does not help you to improve.)

3. Listen deeply. Do not rehearse what you plan to say while others are speaking.

4. Help others feel comfortable when sharing their thoughts and challenges.

5. Be mindful of the protocol and keep the conversation focused.

6. Share the air, and invite silent members into the conversation.

Protocols for Professional Learning Conversations (2nd ed.) by C. Glaude
© 2005, 2011 • solution-tree.com

1.2 Ground Rules for Offering Feedback

1. Listen to the person's need for feedback.

2. Be specific in the feedback.

3. Avoid judgments.

4. Go for quantity.

5. Take time to reflect and sort out what you have heard.

6. Listen with an attitude. Avoid the temptation to rehearse what you plan to say when others are speaking.

Protocols for Professional Learning Conversations (2nd ed.) by C. Glaude
© 2005, 2011 • solution-tree.com

1.3 Ground Rules for Receiving Feedback

1. Keep the spirit of improvement in mind. Direct the feedback.

2. Listen with an attitude to your colleagues' thinking.

3. Be patient and persistent for those valuable insights.

4. Use a protocol.

5. Take time to reflect and sort out what you have heard.

6. Celebrate the ideas offered from your colleagues.

Protocols for Professional Learning Conversations (2nd ed.) by C. Glaude
© 2005, 2011 • solution-tree.com

2.2 Challenging Assumptions	
Column 1	**Column 2**
I think _____ is . . .	I think _____ is NOT . . .

Protocols for Professional Learning Conversations (2nd ed.) by C. Glaude
© 2005, 2011 • solution-tree.com

2.3a Emily's Story: A Vision of Success

Visualize yourself at a particularly important meeting of the school board in the district where you teach. This is the once-a-year meeting at which the district presents the annual report of standardized test scores to the board and the media. Every year it's the same: Will the scores be up or down? How will you compare to national norms? How will your district compare to others in the area?

What most present don't realize as the meeting begins is that, this year, they are in for a big surprise with respect to both the achievement information to be presented and the manner of the presentation.

The audience includes a young woman named Emily, a junior at the high school, sitting in the back of the room with her parents. She knows she will be a big part of the surprise. She's only a little nervous. She understands how important her role is. It has been quite a year for her, unlike any she has ever experienced in school before. She also knows her parents and teacher are as proud of her as she is of herself.

The assistant superintendent begins by reminding the board and the rest of the audience that the district uses standardized tests that sample broad domains of achievement with just a few multiple-choice test items. Much that we value, she points out, must be assessed using other methods. She promises to provide an example later in the presentation. Emily's dad nudges her, and they both smile.

Having set the stage, the assistant superintendent turns to carefully prepared charts depicting average student performance in each important achievement category tested. Results are summarized by grade and building, concluding with a clear description of how district results had changed from the year before and from previous years. As she proceeds, board members ask questions and receive clarification. Some scores are down slightly; some are up. Participants discuss possible reasons. This is a routine annual presentation that proceeds as expected.

Next comes the break from routine. Having completed the first part of the presentation, the assistant superintendent explains how the district has gathered some new information about one important aspect of student achievement. As the board knows, she points out, the district has implemented a new writing program in the high school to address the issue

Stiggins, R. J. (2001). *Student-Involved Classroom Assessment.* 3rd Edition. Upper Saddle River, NJ: Merrill Prentice Hall. Reprinted by permission of Pearson Education, Inc., Upper Saddle River, NJ.

2.3a Emily's Story: A Vision of Success

of poor writing skills among graduates. As part of their preparation for this program, the English faculty attended a summer institute on assessing writing proficiency and integrating such assessments into the teaching and learning process. The English department was confident that this kind of professional development and program revision would produce much higher levels of writing proficiency.

For the second half of the evening's assessment presentation, the high school English department faculty shares the results of their evaluation of the new writing program.

As the very first step in this presentation, the English chair, Ms. Weatherby, who also happens to be Emily's English teacher, distributes a sample of student writing to the board members (with the student's name removed) asking them to read and evaluate this writing. They do so, expressing their dismay aloud as they go. They are indignant in their commentary on these samples of student work. One board member reports in exasperation that, if these represent the results of that new writing program, the community has been had. The board member is right. These are, in fact, pretty weak pieces of work. Emily's mom puts her arm around Emily's shoulder and hugs her.

But Ms. Weatherby urges patience and asks the board to be very specific in stating what they don't like about this work. As the board registers its complaints, the faculty records the criticisms on chart paper for all to see. The list is long, including everything from repetitiveness to disorganization, to short, choppy sentences and disconnected ideas.

Next, the teacher distributes another sample of student writing, asking the board to read and evaluate it. Ah, this, they report, is more like it! This work is much better! But be specific, the chair demands. What do you like about this work? They list positive aspects: good choice of words, sound sentence structure, clever ideas, and so on. Emily is ready to burst! She squeezes her mom's hand.

The reason she's so full of pride at this moment is that this has been a special year for her and her classmates. For the first time ever, they became partners with their English teachers in managing their own improvement as writers. Early in the year, Ms. Weatherby (Ms. W, they all call her) made it crystal clear to Emily that she was, in fact, not a very good writer and that just trying hard to get better was not going to be enough. She expected Emily to be better – nothing else would suffice.

2.3a Emily's Story: A Vision of Success

Ms. W started the year by working with students to set high writing standards, including understanding quality performance in word choice, sentence structure, organization, and voice, and sharing some new analytical scoring guides written just for students. Each explained the differences between good and poor-quality writing in understandable ways. When Emily and her teacher evaluated her first two pieces of writing using these standards, she received very low ratings. Not very good . . .

But she also began to study samples of writing her teacher supplied that Emily could see were very good. Slowly, she began to understand why they were good. The differences between these and her work started to become clear. Ms. W began to share examples and strategies that would help her writing improve one step at a time. As she practiced with these and time passed, Emily and her classmates kept samples of their old writing to compare to their new writing, and they began to build portfolios. Thus, she literally began to watch her own writing skills improve before her very eyes. At midyear, her parents were invited in for a conference at which Emily, not Ms. Weatherby, shared the contents of her portfolio and discussed her emerging writing skills. Emily remembers sharing thoughts about some aspects of her writing that had become very strong and some examples of things she still needed to work on. Now, the year was at an end and here she sat waiting for her turn to speak to the school board about all of this. What a year!

Now, having set the board up by having them analyze, evaluate, and compare these two samples of student work, Ms. W springs the surprise: The two pieces of writing they had just evaluated, one of less sophistication and one of outstanding quality, were produced by the same writer at the beginning and at the end of the school year! This, she reports, is evidence of the kind of impact the new writing program is having on student writing proficiency.

Needless to say, all are impressed. However, one board member wonders aloud, "Have all your students improved in this way?" Having anticipated the question, the rest of the English faculty joins the presentation and produces carefully prepared charts depicting dramatic changes in typical student performance over time on rating scales for each of six clearly articulated dimensions of good writing. They accompany their description of student performance on each scale with actual samples of student work illustrating various levels of proficiency.

Further, Ms. W informs the board that the student whose improvement has been so dramatically illustrated with the work they have analyzed is present at

2.3a Emily's Story: A Vision of Success

this school board meeting, along with her parents. This student is ready to talk with the board about the nature of her learning experience. Emily, you're on!

Interest among the board runs high. Emily talks about how she has come to understand the truly important differences between good and bad writing. She refers to differences she has not understood before, how she has learned to assess her own writing and to fix it when it doesn't work well, and how she and her classmates have learned to talk with her teacher and each other about what it means to write well. Ms. W talks about the improved focus of writing instruction, increase in student motivation, and important positive changes in the very nature of the student–teacher relationship.

A board member asks Emily if she likes to write. She reports, "I do now!" This board member turns to Emily's parents and asks their impression of all of this. They report with pride that they have never seen so much evidence before of Emily's achievement, and most of it came from Emily herself. Emily had never been called on to lead the parent-teacher conference before. They had no idea she was so articulate. They loved it. Their daughter's pride in and accountability for achievement had skyrocketed in the past year.

As the meeting ends, it is clear to all in attendance that evening that this two-part assessment presentation—one part from standardized test scores and one from students, teachers, and the classroom—reveals that assessment is in balance in this district. The test scores cover part of the picture, and classroom assessment evidence completes the achievement picture. There are good feelings all around. The accountability needs of the community are being satisfied and the new writing program is working to improve student achievement. Obviously, this story has a happy ending.

Can you visualize yourself walking out of the boardroom at the end of the evening, hearing parents wishing they had had such an experience in high school? I sure can. Can't you just anticipate the wording of the memo of congratulations the superintendent will soon write to the English department? How about the story that will appear in the newspaper tomorrow, right next to the report of test scores? *Everyone involved here, from Emily to her classmates to parents to teachers to assessment director to (at the end) school board members, understood how to use assessment to promote student success and effective schools.*

2.3b Supporting Evidence	
Key to Success	**Evidence (page number)**

Protocols for Professional Learning Conversations (2nd ed.) by C. Glaude
© 2005, 2011 • solution-tree.com

2.3c Emily's Story: The Keys to Success

What were the active ingredients in this success? To begin with, the faculty understood who is in charge of learning—not them, not the principal, not parents, not school board members, but the students themselves. Therefore, assessment was never a teacher-centered activity, carried out by the teacher to meet the teacher's needs. Rather, it was a student-centered activity, in which Emily and her classmates consistently assessed their own achievement repeatedly over time, so they and their parents could watch the improvement. To be sure, Ms. W controlled writing content and evaluation criteria, and made important decisions based on assessment results. But she also shared the wisdom and power that come from being able to assess the quality of writing. She showed her students the secrets to their own success.

In this way, Ms. W used assessment and its results to build, not destroy, her students' confidence in themselves as writers. The faculty understood that those who believe the target is within reach for them will keep striving. Those who see the target as being beyond reach will give up in hopelessness.

Second, they understood that students can remain self-confident only if they know and understand where they are now in relation to an ultimate vision of success. Ms. W began her program of writing instruction with a highly refined vision of what good writing looks like and shared that vision of excellence with her students from the beginning. Students could continually see the distance closing between their present position and their goal. This turned out to be incredibly empowering for them.

Third, Ms. W and her colleagues knew that their assessments of student achievement had to be very accurate. Writing exercises had to elicit the right kinds of writing. Scoring procedures needed to focus on the important facets of good writing. As faculty members, they needed to train themselves to apply those scoring standards dependably—to avoid making biased judgments about student work.

Stiggins, R. J. (2001). *Student-Involved Classroom Assessment.* 3rd Edition. Upper Saddle River, NJ: Merrill Prentice Hall. Reprinted by permission of Pearson Education, Inc., Upper Saddle River, NJ.

2.3c Emily's Story: The Keys to Success

But, just as important, Ms. W understood that she also had to train her students to make dependable judgments about the quality of their own work. This represents the heart of competence. Any student who cannot evaluate the quality of her own writing and fix it when it isn't working cannot become an independent, lifelong writer.

The final key to success was the great care taken to communicate effectively about student achievement. Whether Ms. W was discussing with Emily improvements needed or achieved in her work or sharing with the school board summary information about average student performance, she took great pains to speak simply, to the point, and with examples to ensure that her meaning was clear.

2.4 Exit Slip

Silently complete this slip at the end of the learning conversation, and submit it to the facilitator as you leave the room.

The feedback may suggest ways to improve the protocol as well as help you frame your learning and next steps.

- What did you learn through this conversation?

- What next steps do you propose for work in this area?

- What suggestions do you have for improving this protocol?

Protocols for Professional Learning Conversations (2nd ed.) by C. Glaude
© 2005, 2011 • solution-tree.com

3.1a The Goal

- Why is this goal important to me?

- How might the work toward this goal improve student learning?

- If I were successful with this goal, what might I see in June?

- What might I collect as evidence of progress toward my goal?

- What resources do I think I will need as I work on this goal?

Protocols for Professional Learning Conversations (2nd ed.) by C. Glaude
© 2005, 2011 • solution-tree.com

3.1b Goal Feedback

- What did I hear this person say about the desired outcome of the goal?

- What am I wondering about with this person's goal?

- What next steps or thoughts came to mind as I heard this person's goal?

- Who might offer help to this person as he or she works on the goal?

Protocols for Professional Learning Conversations (2nd ed.) by C. Glaude
© 2005, 2011 • solution-tree.com

3.7 Unit Plan Guide

1. What are your intended learning targets? Specifically, what essential understandings, knowledge, and/or skills are you attempting to assess in this unit of study?

2. What does evidence of student learning in regard to the intended learning targets look like? What will students need to demonstrate to you?

3. How might you pre-assess your students' learning in regard to the intended learning targets?

4. What methods might you use to assess the learning targets?

5. What instruction might you use to support your assessment?

6. What other things do you need to tell the group about your unit plan?

Protocols for Professional Learning Conversations (2nd ed.) by C. Glaude
© 2005, 2011 • solution-tree.com

4.1 Do You See What I See?

- What questions does this work raise for you?

- What do you think this student is working on?

- What did you learn about how this student thinks and learns?

- What do you think the teacher was attempting to assess?

Protocols for Professional Learning Conversations (2nd ed.) by C. Glaude
© 2005, 2011 • solution-tree.com

4.2 What Is the Goal?

- What is the evidence that the learning result(s) identified are being assessed?

- Is there a match between the learning goals and the assessment method?

- Is the assessment method appropriate for the learning and achievement goals?

- Will the results of this assessment enable students and teachers to determine how successful they were with the learning?

Protocols for Professional Learning Conversations (2nd ed.) by C. Glaude
© 2005, 2011 • solution-tree.com

4.6 Fishbowl Feedback Guidelines

- Stay focused on the evidence that you see in the student's work.

- Avoid judging what you see; merely describe what you see.

- Look openly and broadly; don't let your expectations cloud your views.

- Listen without judgment to what others are saying.

- Focus on understanding different points of view.

- Do not offer background information to various assignments; let the student work speak for itself.

Protocols for Professional Learning Conversations (2nd ed.) by C. Glaude
© 2005, 2011 • solution-tree.com

5.1

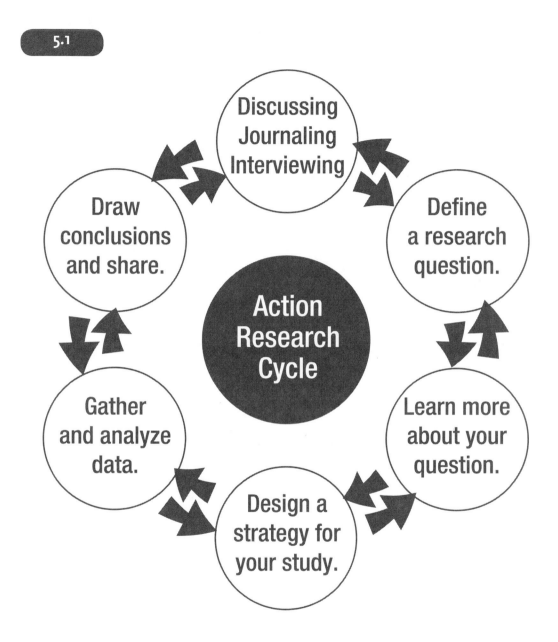

Protocols for Professional Learning Conversations (2nd ed.) by C. Glaude
© 2005, 2011 • solution-tree.com

5.2a Refining the Inquiry Question

- Who will this research affect?

- Why is it important to me?

- What do I want to improve?

- What do I suspect is causing the problem?

- What type of a problem is it?

- What am I proposing to do about it?

- What would I hope to see at the end of my research?

Protocols for Professional Learning Conversations (2nd ed.) by C. Glaude
© 2005, 2011 • solution-tree.com

5.2b Criteria for a High-Quality Action Research Question

- Looks at improving student learning

- Is something a teacher can influence

- Is something a teacher is deeply concerned about

- Is possible with a narrow focus

Protocols for Professional Learning Conversations (2nd ed.) by C. Glaude
© 2005, 2011 • solution-tree.com